JAZZ

THE BLUE SKY PRESS

An Imprint of Scholastic Inc. • New York

on a Saturday Night

LEO & DIANE DILLON

FOR BON, OUR INSPIRATION

And to all the many great jazz musicians, to this unique art form,

and to the spirit of New Orleans.

THE BLUE SKY PRESS

Copyright © 2007 by Leo & Diane Dillon

Library of Congress catalog card number: 2006034009

ISBN 10: 0-590-47893-1 / ISBN 13: 978-0-590-47893-9

10 9 8 7 6 5 4 3 2 1   07 08 09 10 11

Printed in Singapore   46
First printing, September 2007

Designed by Kathleen Westray and Leo & Diane Dillon

Introduction

JAZZ is an original American art form born at the turn of the 20th Century out of blues, ragtime, and marching-band music, with origins in African music. It developed primarily in New Orleans and grew and spread in many American cities such as Kansas City, St. Louis, and Chicago. There are several styles of jazz, which include classic jazz, hot jazz, cool jazz, Dixieland, swing, bebop, and fusion.

The unique quality of jazz is the spontaneous improvisation. Although the musicians may start with a composed score of music, it is used only as a reference point. By the time they have played a round, they have created a completely original piece of music. Surprise is always an element, and often when the musicians are playing, they may hear a particularly brilliant passage and will acknowledge it with a nod or smile. Guest musicians drop in, adding to the excitement.

Although the "Dream Team" in this book never actually happened, most of these musicians performed together at some time in their careers.

This adventurous and exciting art form reached its height of popularity in the 1940s and 1950s, but it is still very much alive and respected around the world.

On stage, the musicians

open their cases,

set up their instruments,

take their places.

Spotlight's on! The announcer sweeps into sight.

"You're in for a session of magic tonight!

Ladies and gents, what a jam this will be—

an evening of jazz immortality!"

The audience hushes.

They worked all week long.

It's their time to hear jazz!

Now along comes a song. . . .

At first, notes surprise; then they sweeten and rise.

Miles Davis on trumpet—sparks heat up the skies.

Toes tapping, hands clapping, now sway left and right,

'cause you move to the music on Saturday night.

Repeat on the beat

when Max Roach keeps the heat

on his drums, rhythm thrums,

makes you jump in your seat.

Jazz is mine! Come along,

won't be long, play my song.

Fills my soul—makes me whole—

jazz is mine! I belong. . . .

Charlie Parker on alto sax—

don't need a word. . . .

Notes fly through the sky

on the wings of a bird.

Take that tune, shake the moon—

John Coltrane on *his* sax.

His sax talks to Charlie's,

and Charlie's talks back.

A river of melody

sketched in dim light.

Catch the excitement

on Saturday night.

Thelonious Monk invents on the keys,

does his own thing—not aiming to please.

Discordant chords now blend to be

pure genius, joined in harmony.

A guest with guitar—lightning fingers begin. . . .

He takes strings for a walk, strings can talk, now he's in.

The musicians smile with a meeting of eyes.

A cool night, a cool note—they all improvise.

On bass, Stanley Clarke

plucking sweet mellow tones—

feel the vibrations

deep down in your bones.

Now Ella Fitzgerald sings bebop doo-wop!

Can't hold still, get our fill, never will, please don't stop!

Let your heart go, let it soar like a kite. . . .

We explode in applause, on our feet with delight.

The curtain is closed, but we still hold the glow.

Feel the beat in your feet, what a treat, time to go.

Come again, tell us when, it was all outta sight!

Jazz is so cool on a Saturday night.

The Musicians

MILES DAVIS (1926–1991) TRUMPET

Miles grew up in East St. Louis, Illinois. Early on, his mother wanted him to play the violin, but he was given a trumpet as a boy, and that sealed his fate. Miles was playing trumpet professionally by age fifteen. After playing in various groups and recording his music, he formed his own group, the Miles Davis Quintet, which later became a sextet. Many consider him the most innovative jazz musician from the 1940s to the 1960s. His sensational improvisations brought him fame.

MAX ROACH (1925–) DRUMS

Max grew up in Brooklyn, New York, and his mother was a gospel singer. He began playing in a band at the age of ten. In grammar school, he often took home instruments to practice. He first came into prominence during the birth of modern jazz as a drummer, recording with Dizzy Gillespie and Coleman Hawkins, then joining Charlie Parker's band. He was involved in the freedom movement of the 1960s and also composed music for dance, theater, film, and television.

CHARLIE PARKER (1920–1955) ALTO SAXOPHONE

From the age of seven, Charlie grew up in Kansas City, Missouri. He had his first music lessons in public school and began playing the saxophone at the age of eleven. At fourteen he played his first professional gig. He developed his unique style of playing through jam sessions, by listening to great musicians of his time, and also through the process of trial and error. He was nicknamed "Bird," and the famous New York jazz club, Birdland, was named after him.

JOHN COLTRANE (1926–1967) TENOR & SOPRANO SAXOPHONE

John grew up in North Carolina and learned to play an instrument at the age of thirteen. He started out playing clarinet, but when he became interested in jazz, he switched to the saxophone. He performed with numerous groups and was a bandleader and composer. He reached a peak of fame in the mid-1950s when he played with the Miles Davis Quintet. John had a powerful influence on jazz and inspired an entire generation of jazz musicians.

THELONIOUS MONK (1917–1982) PIANO

Thelonious grew up in New York City, which remained his home until he retired. He performed with many groups and toured the United States and Europe. A brilliant innovator, he also recorded with several record companies. Although he remained less known and less understood by the general public for many years, he became famous for his controversial jazz improvisations and was highly respected by his fellow musicians.

STANLEY CLARKE (1951–) ACOUSTIC & ELECTRIC BASS

As a young person, Stanley played accordion, then moved on to violin, and later tried cello. He finally decided the bass was the instrument for him. He attended the Philadelphia Academy of Music and studied jazz, post-bop, fusion, and jazz funk. By the age of twenty-five, he was already called a legend and a celebrated pioneer in fusion jazz music. He also created music scores for television and film.

ELLA FITZGERALD (1918–1996) VOICE

Ella grew up in Yonkers, New York. She considered herself a tomboy and loved sports. In 1934, as a teenager, she entered an amateur contest sponsored by the Apollo Theater in Harlem, New York City, and the rest is history. She was shy and self-conscious, but on stage she had no fear. She is most famous for her improvised "scat" solos. Her voice was flexible and had a wide range, and she could imitate many instruments.

Some of our favorite jazz recordings featuring these musicians:

MILES DAVIS—*Dear Old Stockholm; In a Silent Way; Sketches of Spain*

MAX ROACH—*Friendship; Money Jungle; We Insist! Freedom Now*

CHARLIE PARKER—*Ah-Leu-Cha; Cherokee; I Remember You*

JOHN COLTRANE—*A Love Supreme; Giant Steps; My Favorite Things*

THELONIOUS MONK—*Blue Monk; 'Round About Midnight; Ruby, My Dear*

STANLEY CLARKE—*Minute by Minute; School Days; Time Exposure*

ELLA FITZGERALD—*A Tisket, A Tasket; It Ain't Necessarily So; Summertime*

(SOURCES AVAILABLE UPON REQUEST.)

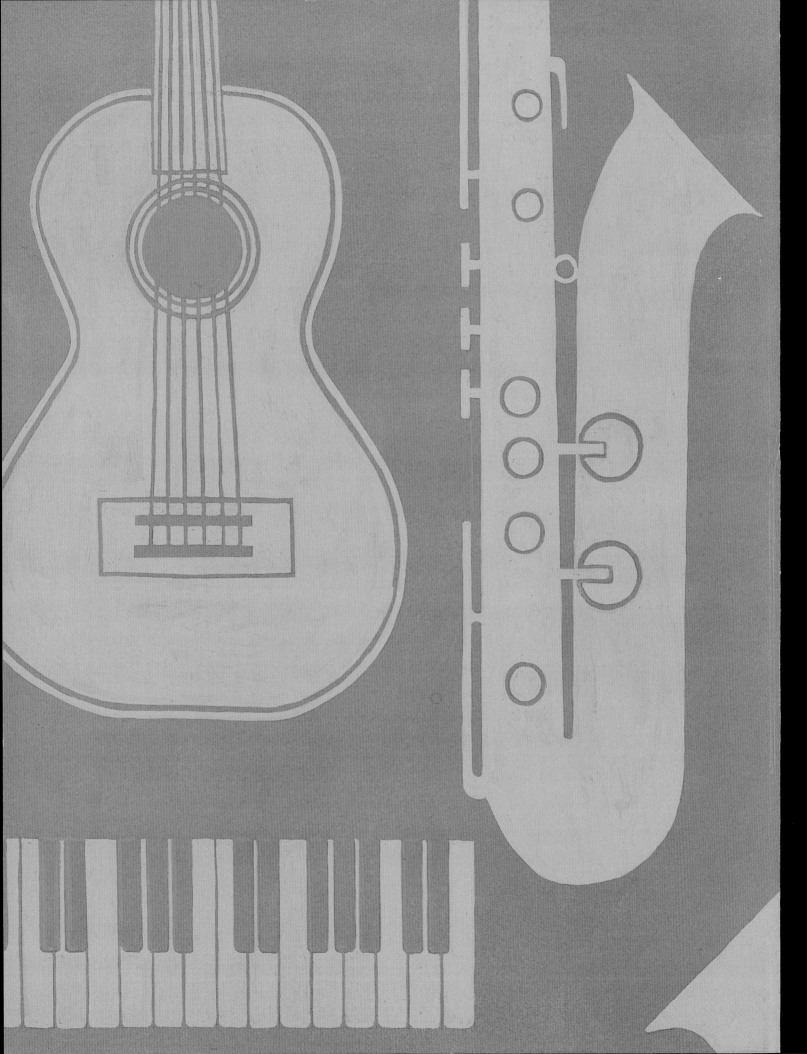